Carry your stuff with unique style! This bag collection
shapes and sizes, with pattern options to reflect y

25

16

6

LEISURE ARTS, INC. • Maumelle, Arkansas

Travel light and still take your little necessities: art supplies, cell phone, GPS handheld device (hey, you never know when the urge to go geocaching will strike). Since this itty-bitty bag is quick to make, you should probably have several in different colors.

Mini Bag

Design by Kristine Poor

Finished size: 6½" x 9" x 2½" (17 cm x 23 cm x 6 cm)

SHOPPING LIST

Yardage is based on 43"/44" (109 cm/112 cm) wide fabric.

- ☐ ¼ yd (23 cm) of blue floral fabric
- ☐ ⅜ yd (34 cm) of purple polka dot fabric
- ☐ ⅜ yd (34 cm) of lining fabric
- ☐ 3½" x 3½" (9 cm x 9 cm) square each of 3 coordinating fabrics for front flap

You will also need:

- ☐ 16" x 31" (41 cm x 79 cm) rectangle of lightweight batting (we used Warm and Natural®)
- ☐ 1½ yds (1.4 m) of ¼" (6 mm) dia. braided cord for strap
- ☐ Quilt basting spray
- ☐ Hook and loop closure (optional)

CUTTING THE PIECES

*Follow **Rotary Cutting**, page 40, to cut fabric. Cut all strips across the selvage-to-selvage width of the fabric. All measurements include ¹/₄" seam allowances.*

From blue floral fabric:
- Cut 1 strip 6½" wide. From this strip, cut 1 **outer fabric rectangle** 20" x 6½" and 1 **bag side rectangle** and 1 **bag side lining rectangle**, each 10" x 6".

From purple polka dot fabric:
- Cut 2 **binding strips** 2½" wide.
- Cut 1 **square** 3½" x 3½".
- Cut 1 **flap top** 2½" x 6½".

From lining fabric:
- Cut 1 **bag lining** 29½" x 8½".

From batting:
- Cut 1 **large batting rectangle** 29½" x 8½".
- Cut 1 **small batting rectangle** 10" x 6".

MAKING THE FOUR-PATCH BLOCK

*Follow **Sewing**, page 41, and **Pressing**, page 42. Match right sides and raw edges and use a ¹/₄" seam allowance.*

1. Sew 2 **squares** together to make **Unit 1**. Make 2 Unit 1's.

Unit 1 (make 2)

2. Sew the 2 Unit 1's together to make a **Four-Patch Block.**

Four-Patch Block

3

MAKING THE MINI BAG SECTIONS

1. Sew **Four-Patch Block**, **flap top**, and **outer fabric rectangle** together to make **outer bag** (**Fig. 1**). Press seam allowances open.

Fig. 1

2. Refer to **Making Quilted Fabric**, page 42, to layer and quilt as desired using **outer bag**, **large batting rectangle**, and **bag lining**.

Quilting Tip: Our fabric is quilted with an X through the center of the Four-Patch Block. There is outline quilting inside the triangles formed by the X. The flap top is meander quilted and there is diagonal crosshatching on the remainder of the outer bag.

3. Trim backing and batting even with edges of quilted fabric. Trimming length from outer fabric rectangle end, trim quilted fabric to 27½" x 6½" to make **bag body**.

4. Using rounded corner of **Mini Bag side pattern** as a guide, trim both corners of the Four-Patch Block end of bag body (**Fig. 2**).

Fig. 2

5. Refer to **Making Binding**, page 43, to use **binding strips** to make binding. Set binding aside.

6. To bind short *straight* edge of bag body, use binding and follow **Attaching Open End Binding**, page 44.

7. Make quilted fabric in the same manner as above, using **bag side rectangle**, **small batting rectangle**, and **bag side lining rectangle**.

Quilting Tip: Our fabric is quilted with an allover meandering pattern.

8. Using **Mini Bag side pattern**, cut 2 **bag sides** from quilted fabric (**Fig. 3**).

Fig. 3

ASSEMBLING THE MINI BAG

1. Referring to **Fig. 4,** mark center bottom of bag body with dots placed 9¾" from bound edge and ¼" from each side edge (**Fig. 4**).

Fig. 4

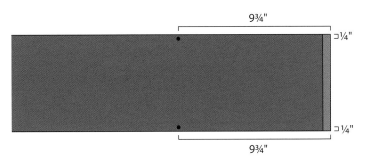

2. Mark center bottom of each bag side with a dot (**Fig. 5**).

Fig. 5

3. On lining side, pin 1 raw end of **strap** to center of each short straight edge of bag side; stitch across strap ends ¹/₄" below raw edges (**Fig. 6**).

Fig. 6

4. To bind short *straight* edges of bag sides using prepared binding, follow **Attaching Open End Binding**, page 44.
5. With lining sides together and matching dots, sew sides to bag body.
6. To bind seam allowances along side, flap, and remaining side using prepared binding, begin at top edge of bag opening and follow **Attaching Closed End Binding**, page 44.
7. **Optional:** Attach hook and loop fastener to flap and bag body.

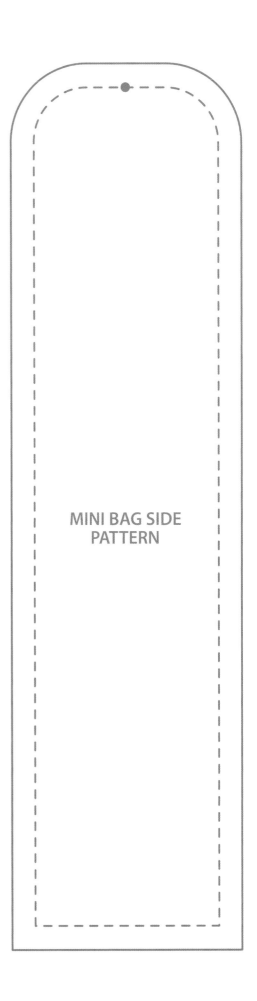

MINI BAG SIDE
PATTERN

Adjustable shoulder strap, handy side pocket, interior pocket for smaller items, gerbera daisies dotting a sunny background: Be sure to make an extra one of these beauties for your friends to borrow, because you know they're going to ask. Also looks fabulous in the fabric of your choice.

Shoulder Bag

Design by Kristine Poor

Finished Size: 12" x 9½" x 2" (30 cm x 24 cm x 5 cm)

SHOPPING LIST

Yardage is based on 43"/44" (109 cm/112 cm) wide fabric.

- ☐ 1⅞ yds (1.7 m) of yellow floral fabric
- ☐ 8" x 8" (20 cm x 20 cm) piece of yellow print fabric for star points
- ☐ 6" x 3" (15 cm x 8 cm) piece of orange print fabric for star centers
- ☐ ⅛ yd (11 cm) of pink print fabric

You will also need:

- ☐ 31½" x 28" (80 cm x 71 cm) rectangle of lightweight batting (we used Warm and Natural®)
- ☐ 12½" x 14" (32 cm x 36 cm) rectangle of lightweight fusible interfacing
- ☐ ⅛ yd (11 cm) of Pellon® Peltex®70 heavyweight interfacing
- ☐ Two 1½" (38 mm) D rings
- ☐ 9" (23 cm) plastic zipper
- ☐ Quilt basting spray

CUTTING THE PIECES

*Follow **Rotary Cutting**, page 40, to cut fabric. Cut all strips across the selvage-to-selvage width of the fabric. All measurements include ¼" seam allowances.*

From yellow floral fabric:
- Cut 1 **lining** 26" x 20".
- Cut 1 **pocket lining** 14½" x 9½".
- Cut 2 **front/back rectangles** 13" x 11".
- Cut 1 **inner pocket** 12½" x 14".
- Cut 1 **long strap** 4½" x 38⅝".
- Cut 1 **short strap** 4½" x 14⅞".
- Cut 2 **upper zipper facings** 1⅜" x 11".
- Cut 2 **lower zipper facings** 1¼" x 11".
- Cut 1 **bottom rectangle** 3½" x 12".
- Cut 6 **small squares** 2" x 2".
- Cut 8 **medium squares** 2½" x 2½".
- Cut 8 **large squares** 2⅞" x 2⅞".
- Cut 5 **binding strips** 2½" x 18".

From yellow print fabric:
- Cut 8 **rectangles** 1¾" x 3¼".

From orange print fabric:
- Cut 2 **medium squares** 2½" x 2½".

From pink print fabric:
- Cut 1 **pocket binding strip** 2" x 13".
- Cut 6 **small squares** 2" x 2".

From batting:
- Cut 1 **batting rectangle** 26" x 20".
- Cut 1 **pocket batting** 14½" x 9½".

From heavyweight interfacing:
- Cut 2 **long strap interfacings** 1¼" x 19".
- Cut 1 **short strap interfacing** 1¼" x 14¼".

MAKING THE OUTER POCKET

*Follow **Sewing**, page 41, and **Pressing**, page 42. Match right sides and raw edges and use a ¼" seam allowance.*

Triangle-Square Strip

1. Referring to **Making Triangle-Squares**, page 41, use 6 yellow floral **small squares** and 6 pink print **small squares** to make 12 **Triangle-Squares**. Trim Triangle-Squares to 1½" x 1½".

Triangle-Square (make 12)

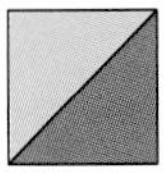

2. Sew 6 Triangle-Squares together to form a **Triangle-Square Strip**. Make 2 Triangle-Square Strips. Set Triangle-Square Strips aside.

Triangle-Square Strip (make 2)

Star Block

1. Mark a dot at center top edge of 1 yellow floral **large square**. Draw a line from center dot to each bottom corner of square (**Fig. 1**). Cut along drawn line to make 1 **center triangle**. Repeat with remaining large squares to make 8 center triangles.

Fig. 1

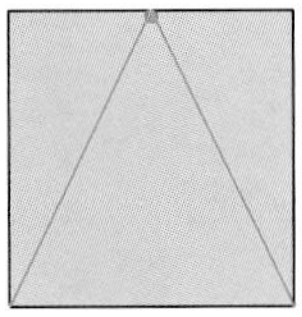

Center Triangle (make 8)

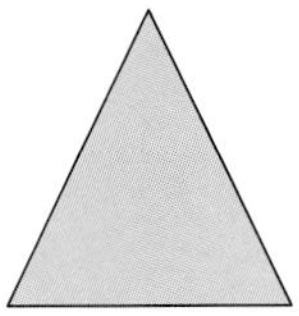

2. Draw a diagonal line from top left to bottom right corners on 4 yellow print **rectangles** (**Fig. 2**). Draw a diagonal line from top right to bottom left corners on remaining yellow print **rectangles** (**Fig. 3**). Cut along drawn lines to make 8 **right side triangles** and 8 **left side triangles**.

Fig. 2

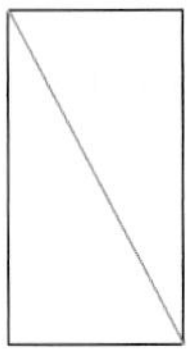

Fig. 3

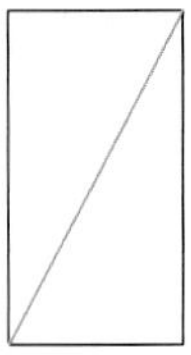

Right Side Triangle
(make 8)

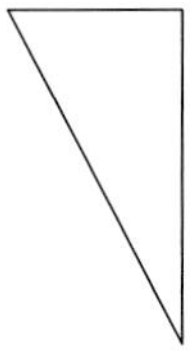

Left Side Triangle
(make 8)

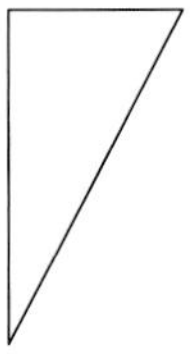

3. Referring to **Fig. 4**, match top points of triangles to sew 1 right side triangle to 1 center triangle. Repeat to sew 1 left side triangle to opposite side of center triangle to make a **star point.** Trim star point to 2½" x 2½". Make 8 star points.

Fig. 4

Star Point
(make 8)

4. Sew 4 yellow floral **medium squares**, 4 star points, and 1 orange print **medium square** together to make **Star Block.** Make 2 Star Blocks.

Star Block (make 2)

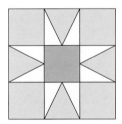

5. Sew 1 **Triangle-Square Strip** to 1 edge of each Star Block (**Fig. 5**).

Fig. 5

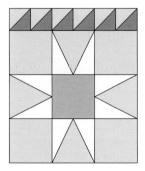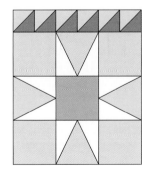

6. Referring to **Fig. 6** for orientation, sew Star Blocks together to make **front pocket**.

Fig. 6

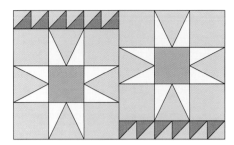

7. Refer to **Making Quilted Fabric**, page 42, to layer and quilt as desired using **front pocket**, **pocket batting**, and **pocket lining**.

Quilting Tip: Our front pocket is quilted in the ditch along all the seamlines. There is an X quilted across the center of each star.

8. Trim batting and lining even with edges of front pocket.
9. Matching wrong sides and raw edges, press **pocket binding strip** in half lengthwise.
10. Refer to **Attaching Open End Binding**, page 44, to bind 1 long edge of front pocket using pocket binding strip. This will be the top of your front pocket. Set front pocket aside.

PREPARING THE QUILTED SECTIONS

1. Refer to **Making Quilted Fabric**, page 42, to layer and quilt as desired using **front/back rectangles** and **bottom rectangles, batting rectangle,** and **lining** (**Fig. 7**).

Fig. 7

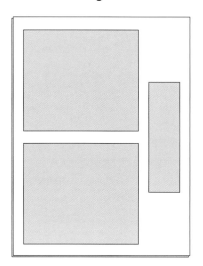

Quilting Tip: Our fabric is quilted with an allover meandering pattern.

2. Trim each front/back rectangle to 12½" x 10½". Use **Shoulder Bag front/back pattern**, page 14, to trim top and side edges of 1 front/back rectangle to make **front** (**Fig. 8**). Repeat for remaining front/back rectangle to make **back**.

Fig. 8

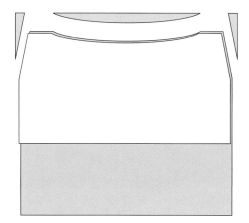

3. Matching wrong side of pocket to right side of front, align raw edges of front pocket with bottom and side edges of front. Baste around pocket, ¼" from side and bottom edges. Beginning with backstitching at bound edge of pocket, stitch in the ditch between Star Blocks to make 2 pocket sections.
4. Use **Shoulder Bag bottom pattern**, page 15, to cut 1 **bottom** from bottom rectangle.
5. Set front, back, and bottom aside.

PREPARING THE INNER POCKET

1. Fuse **lightweight fusible interfacing rectangle** to wrong side of **inner pocket**.
2. Matching wrong sides and short edges, fold inner pocket in half; press.
3. Press folded edge over ⅜" to one side and topstitch in place. The topstitched side will be the right side of inner pocket.
4. Matching lining side of back and wrong side of pocket, place inner pocket on back. Align long and short raw edges of inner pocket with bottom and side edges of back. Sew inner pocket to back ¼" from sides and bottom edges (**Fig. 9**).

Fig. 9

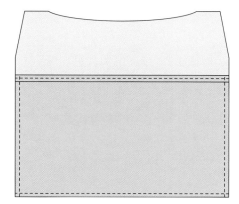

PREPARING THE ZIPPER ASSEMBLY

1. Press 1 long edge of each **lower** and **upper zipper facing** ½" to wrong side.
2. With closed zipper wrong side up, position pressed edge of 1 lower zipper facing on zipper tape ¼" away from teeth; pin facing in place. Topstitch ⅛" from folded edge of facing (**Fig. 10**).

Fig. 10

3. With closed zipper right side up, position pressed edge of 1 upper zipper facing over zipper tape and lower facing about ⅛" away from teeth; pin facing in place. Topstitch ⅛" from folded edge (**Fig. 11**).

Fig. 11

4. Repeat **Steps 2-3** to sew remaining zipper facings to opposite side of zipper to make **zipper assembly**.
5. Referring to **Fig. 12**, trim zipper assembly to 10" long as shown. Set zipper assembly aside.

Fig. 12

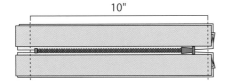

PREPARING THE STRAPS

1. Press 1 long and 1 short edge of **long** and **short strap** ⅝" to wrong side.
2. Cut 1 **long strap interfacing** in half to make two 1½" x 9½" pieces.
3. Arrange 1 long and 2 short interfacing pieces together as shown. Butt (do not overlap) short edges and zigzag ends together (**Fig. 13**).

Fig. 13

4. On wrong side of long strap, align 1 long edge of 1 long strap interfacing with long un-pressed edge of strap. Tuck 1 short end of interfacing under folded short end. Stitch in place ¼" from long edge (**Fig. 14**).

Fig. 14

5. Fold interfacing over once, then fold pressed edge of fabric over interfacing (**Figs. 15-16**).

Fig. 15   **Fig. 16**

6. Beginning and ending at short raw end, topstitch strap close to folded edge along both long edges and across short finished edge. Topstitch again ⅛" on either side of first topstitching line (**Fig. 17**).

Fig. 17

7. Repeat **Steps 4-6** using short strap and short strap interfacing.

8. Attach D-rings to long strap by placing finished end of strap through D-rings. Fold end of strap 1¾" to the wrong side and topstitch in place (**Fig. 18**). Set straps aside.

Fig. 18

ASSEMBLING THE BAG

1. Refer to **Making Binding**, page 43, to use **binding strips** to make **binding**. Set binding aside.

2. Matching right sides, sew raw end of long strap to zipper pull end of zipper assembly. Sew raw end of short strap to opposite end of zipper assembly (**Fig. 19**).

Fig. 19

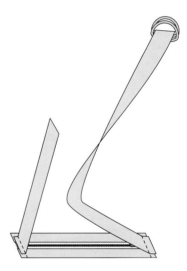

3. Matching right sides and easing as needed, sew 1 edge of zipper assembly to curved top edge of back (**Fig. 20**). Sew remaining side of zipper assembly to curved top edge of front.

Fig. 20

4. Refer to **Attaching Open End Binding**, page 44, to use prepared binding to bind curved top edge seam allowances.

5. Matching right sides and tucking straps between layers, sew front and back together along side edges (**Fig. 21**). Refer to **Attaching Open End Binding**, page 44, to use prepared binding to bind side seam allowances.

Fig. 21

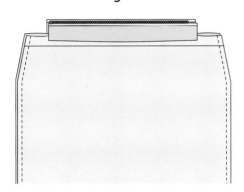

6. Matching right sides, align center of zipper assembly with side seam (**Fig. 22**); sew across end.

Fig. 22

7. Refer to **Attaching Closed End Binding**, page 44, to use prepared binding to bind end.

8. To attach **bottom**, match right sides and align dots on **bottom** with side seams on lower edge of bag body; pin (**Fig. 23**). Easing as needed, sew bottom to bag body.

Fig. 23

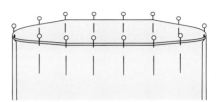

9. Refer to **Attaching Continuous Binding**, page 44, to use prepared binding to bind bottom seam allowances. Turn bag right side out.

SHOULDER BAG
FRONT/BACK PATTERN

To trace a complete pattern, trace half the pattern onto tracing paper using a pen or pencil with dark lead. Fold tracing paper in half along fold line, flip paper to unmarked side and trace along previously drawn lines.

Fold

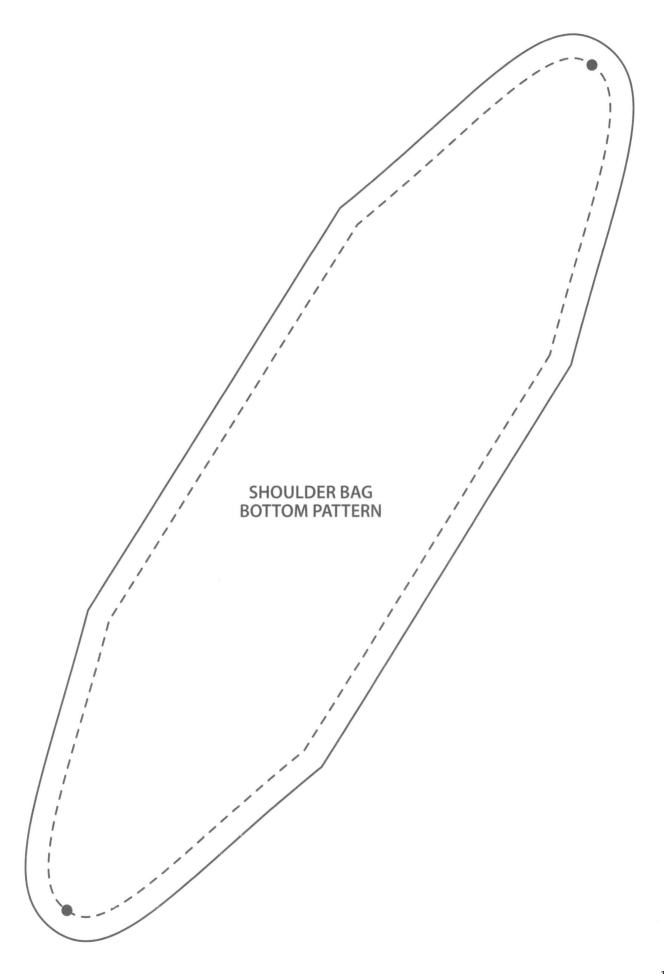

SHOULDER BAG
BOTTOM PATTERN

They're not just for schoolbooks and trail mix anymore, but if that's why you want a backpack, this classic bag can take care of those jobs, too. Details include a drawstring and flap closure, handy finger loop, and D-ring straps. There's even an inner pocket for items that need extra stability, like water bottles or small electronics.

Floral Stripe Backpack

Design by Kristine Poor
Finished Size: 10" x 15" x 6" (25 cm x 38 cm x 15 cm)

SHOPPING LIST

Yardage is based on 43"/44" (109 cm/112 cm) wide fabric.

- ☐ 1½ yds (1.4 m) of floral stripe fabric*
- ☐ 1½ yds (1.4 m) of blue polka dot fabric
- ☐ ⅞ yd (80 cm) of green tone-on-tone fabric

You will also need:

- ☐ 32½" x 38" (83 cm x 97 cm) rectangle of lightweight batting (we used Warm and Natural®)
- ☐ ⅝ yd (57 cm) of 20" (51 cm) wide Pellon® 70 Peltex® Sew-In Ultra-Firm Stabilizer
- ☐ Quilt basting spray
- ☐ Four 1½" (38 mm) D rings
- ☐ ¾ yd (69 cm) of ¼" (6 mm) dia. twisted cord for drawstring
- ☐ Tape in a color to match drawstring cord
- ☐ Two 1" (25 mm) long cord stops

* We used a fabric with a combination of wide and narrow print and solid stripes. For the front/side of our backpack, we cut a length of fabric that included 1 wide and 2 narrow stripes. For the flap we cut a length that included 1 medium and 2 narrow stripes. Because the stripe lengths are sewn to the top of the backpack fabric for decorative purposes only, your lengths can be cut wider or narrower depending on the width and number of stripes you want to feature. For the casings, we cut lengths of the narrow stripe. You will need to cut a section of fabric wide enough for the cord to fit through the casings.

CUTTING THE PIECES

*Follow **Rotary Cutting**, page 40, to cut fabric. Cut all strips across the selvage-to-selvage width of the fabric. All measurements include ¼" seam allowances.*

From floral stripe fabric:
- Cut 1 **front/side accent** 24" x desired stripe width + ¼" seam allowance on each long edge.
- Cut 1 **flap accent** 11" x desired stripe width + ¼" seam allowance on each long edge.
- Cut 1 **front/side/bottom lining** 26" x 23½".
- Cut 1 **flap lining** 13" x 13½".
- Cut 2 **long casings** 12" x 2", cut on desired stripe.
- Cut 1 **short casing** 1½" x 2", cut on desired stripe.
- Cut 1 **loop** 6" x 1".

From blue polka dot fabric:
- Cut 1 **front/side** 24" x 15".
- Cut 2 **upper straps** 22⅝" x 4½".
- Cut 2 **lower straps** 20⅝" x 4½".
- Cut 1 **inner pocket** 7" x 18".
- Cut 1 **back** 11" x 14½".
- Cut 1 **flap** 11" x 11½".
- Cut 1 **bottom** 11" x 6¾".
- Cut 2 **strap covers** 5" x 3".

From green tone-on-tone fabric:
- Cut 4 **binding strips** 2½" wide.
- Cut 2 **front trim strips** 24" x 2".
- Cut 1 **back lining** 13" x 16½".
- Cut 2 **flap trim strips** 11" x 2".
- Cut 1 **back trim strip** 11" x ¾".

From batting:
- Cut 1 **back batting** 13" x 16½".
- Cut 1 **flap batting** 13" x 13½".
- Cut 1 **front/side/bottom batting** 26" x 23½".

From interfacing:
- Cut 2 **lower strap interfacings** 20" x 1¼".
- Cut 2 **upper strap interfacings** 22" x 1¼".

PREPARING THE QUILTED SECTIONS

*Follow **Sewing**, page 41, and **Pressing**, page 42. Match right sides and raw edges and use a ¼" seam allowance.*

1. Mark center of 1 long edge of **front/side**. Mark center of 1 long edge of **bottom**.
2. Matching center marks, sew front/side and bottom together (**Fig. 1**). Press seam allowance toward **front/side**.

Fig. 1

3. Refer to **Making Quilted Fabric**, page 42, to layer and quilt as desired using **front/side/bottom lining**, **front/side/bottom batting**, and **front/side/bottom**.

Quilting Tip: Our fabric is quilted with an allover meandering pattern.

4. Trim lining and batting even with edges of front/side/bottom.
5. Repeat **Steps 3-4** using **flap lining**, **flap batting**, and **flap**.

Quilting Tip: Our flap is quilted with a diagonal grid pattern.

6. Repeat **Steps 3-4** using **back lining**, **back batting**, and **back**.

Quilting Tip: Our back is quilted with a diagonal grid pattern.

ATTACHING THE TRIM AND ACCENT STRIPS

1. Matching wrong sides, press **front trim strips** and **flap trim strips** in half lengthwise.
2. Sew 1 front trim strip to each long right side edge of **front/side accent** (**Fig. 2**) and 1 flap trim strip to each long right side edge of **flap accent** (**Fig. 3**).

Fig. 2

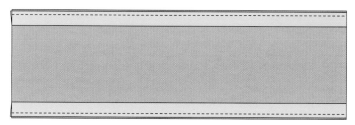

Fig. 3

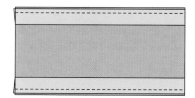

3. Press front and flap trim strips away from front and flap accents (**Fig. 4**).

Fig. 4

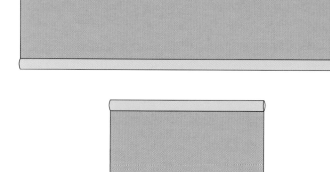

4. Position 1 edge of flap accent 1" from 1 short raw edge of flap. Using a walking foot, topstitch in place close to folded edge of flap accent. Repeat for remaining folded edge (**Fig. 5**). If needed, trim ends of accent strips even with edges of flap.

Fig. 5

Quilting Tip: We added quilting lines to the flap using the stripes in the fabric as a guide.

5. Repeat **Step 4** to attach front/side accent 1" above seamline on front/side/bottom.

Quilting Tip: We added quilting lines to the flap using the stripes in the fabric as a guide.

PREPARING STRAPS, STRAP COVER, AND LOOP

1. Press 1 long and 1 short edge of each **upper** and **lower strap** ⅝" to wrong side.
2. On wrong side of 1 upper strap, align 1 long edge of 1 **upper strap interfacing** with long unpressed edge of strap. Tuck 1 short end of interfacing under folded short end. Stitch in place ¼" from long edge (**Fig. 6**).

Fig. 6

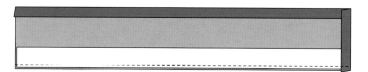

3. Fold interfacing over once, then fold pressed edge of handle over interfacing (**Figs. 7-8**).

Fig. 7   **Fig. 8**

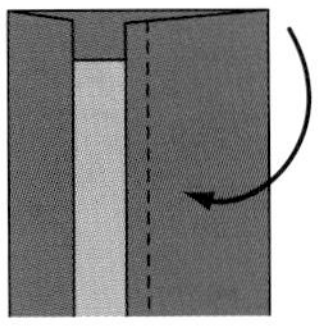

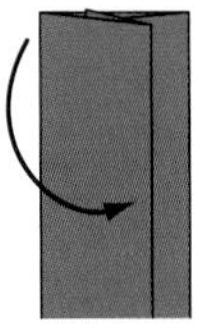

4. Topstitch handle in place close to folded edge. Topstitch along length of opposite side of handle. Topstitch ⅛" outside each topstitching line (**Fig. 9**).

Fig. 9

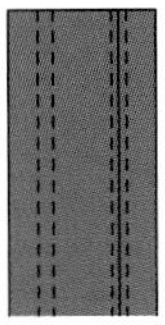

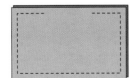

5. Repeat **Steps 2-4** using remaining upper strap and upper strap interfacing and lower straps and lower strap interfacings.

6. Attach D-rings to the upper straps by placing finished end of strap through D-rings. Fold end of strap 2¼" to the wrong side and topstitch in place (**Fig. 10**).

Fig. 10

7. Leaving an opening for turning, sew **strap covers** together along all 4 sides (**Fig. 11**). Turn to right side; press.

Fig. 11

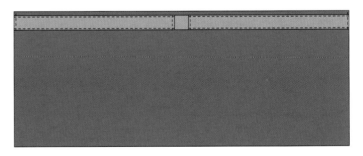

8. Press each edge of **loop** ¼" to the wrong side. Matching wrong sides, fold loop in half lengthwise and topstitch folded edges together.

ASSEMBLING THE BACKPACK

1. Press both long edges of each **long casing** ¼" to wrong side. Press 1 short edge ¼" to wrong side twice. To hem, topstitch across each pressed short edge.

2. Press both long edges of **short casing** ¼" to wrong side. Mark center of top edge of front/side/bottom. Center short casing over front/side/bottom center mark ¼" from top edge and top stitch in place along pressed edges (**Fig. 12**).

Fig. 12

3. With hemmed short edges over short casing, pin long casings to front/side ¼" below top edge. Topstitch in place along pressed edges (**Fig. 13**).

Fig. 13

4. Fold **drawstring** in half to find and mark center. To prevent cord from fraying, wrap a length of tape around drawstring on either side of center mark. Cut drawstring in half at center mark. Insert 1 drawstring through each casing. To secure, stitch across ends at side edges (**Fig. 14**).

Fig. 14

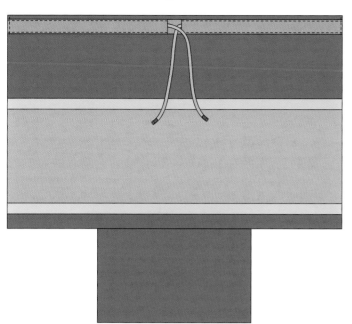

Strap Diagram

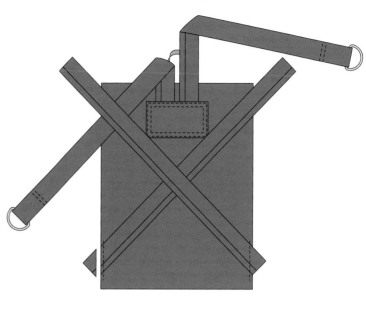

5. Mark center top on 1 short edge of back. With ends of loop even with top raw edge, baste loop to right side of back about ⅜" on either side of center mark (**Fig. 15**).

Fig. 15

6. Referring to **Strap Diagram**, center and sew raw ends of upper straps to right side of back 3" below top edge.

7. Center strap cover over raw ends of upper straps and topstitch in place around all 4 sides. Topstitch again ¼" inside previous stitching.

8. Position raw ends of lower straps at a 45° angle, 1" above bottom edge of back. Stitch in place. Trim ends of straps even with side edges of back.

9. To make inner pocket, match wrong sides and short ends and fold **inner pocket** in half. Fold lower folded edge up 4" (**Fig. 16**). Baste layers together along sides.

Fig. 16

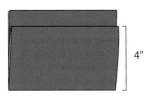

4"

10. Refer to **Making Binding**, page 43, to make **binding** using **binding strips**.
11. To bind side edges of pocket, refer to **Attaching Closed End Binding**, page 44, for lower edges and **Attaching Open End Binding**, page 44, for upper edges.

12. Center top edge of pocket on upper edge of lining side of back. Baste in place along upper edge.
13. Matching right sides and top raw edges, sew back and flap together. Refer to **Attaching Open End Binding**, page 44, to use prepared binding to bind top edge of back.
14. Press under both long edges of **back trim strip** ¼" to the wrong side. Press loop toward flap. On right side of back, position back trim strip over seam and loop ends. Topstitch along both pressed edges of trim strip.
15. Matching right sides, sew 1 side edge of bottom to 1 bottom edge of front/side (**Fig. 17**). Repeat for remaining side. Refer to **Attaching Closed End Binding**, page 44, to use prepared binding to bind seam end at front of backpack and **Attaching Open end Binding**, page 44, to bind seam end at back of backpack.

Fig. 17

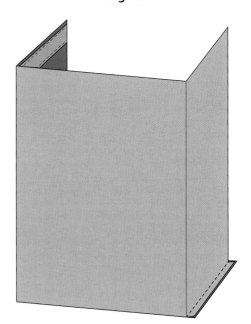

16. Matching right sides, refer to **Fig. 18** to pin then sew back to front/side around all 3 sides. Refer to **Attaching Open End Binding**, page 44, to use prepared binding to bind seam allowances.

Fig. 18

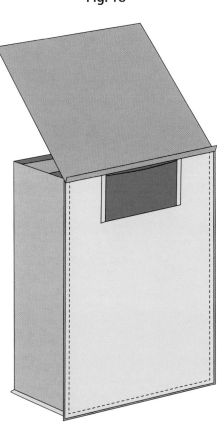

17. Referring to **Fig. 19**, use a small drinking glass (approximately 3" in diameter) to round corners of flap.

Fig. 19

18. Refer to **Attaching Continuous Binding**, page 44, to use prepared binding to bind remaining raw edges of top edge and flap (**Fig. 20**).

Fig. 20

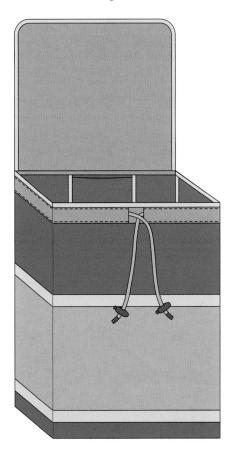

19. To attach cord stops to drawstring ends, depress top of cord stop and thread 1 drawstring end through hole. Repeat for remaining cord stop and drawstring.

This pattern is designed to utilize charm squares. All the totes have a cute cuff on the outside, pockets on the inside, and an optional drawstring closure. The pattern also gives you 3 options for the front and back of the tote. One tote features a little pocket that's perfect for your cell phone, one tote features charm squares turned on point, and one tote features dimensional pinwheels.

Pinwheel Tote

3 Charming Totes

Designs by Sue Marsh

Finished Size: 13 1/2"w x 13 1/2"h x 4 1/2"d
(34 cm x 34 cm x 11 cm)

SHOPPING LIST

Fabric yardage is based on 43"/44" (109 cm/112 cm) wide fabric with a usable width of 40" (102 cm). Fat quarters measure approximately 21" x 18" (53 cm x 46 cm). Charm squares measure 5" x 5" (13 cm x 13 cm).

For all totes:
- ☐ 1/4 yd (23 cm) of fabric #1 **or** 1 fat quarter for cuff
- ☐ 7/8 yd (80 cm) of fabric #2 for lining and inside pocket
- ☐ 1 yd (91 cm) of 20" (51 cm) wide fusible interfacing (such as Pellon® Shape-Flex® SF 101)
- ☐ 7/8 yd (80 cm) of 44" (112 cm) wide fusible fleece (such as Pellon® Fusible Thermolam® Plus)
- ☐ 3/8 yd (34 cm) of fabric #3 **or** 1 fat quarter for drawstring closure (optional)
- ☐ 2 yds (1.8 m) of cord or ribbon for drawstring (optional)
- ☐ water-soluble fabric marking pen

For Pocket Tote, you will also need:
- ☐ 41 charm squares for front, back, sides, bottom, and handle*
- ☐ Eight 9/16" (14 mm) dia. buttons

For Charms-On-Point Tote, you will also need:
- ☐ 37 charm squares for front, back, sides, bottom, and handle*
- ☐ 3/8 yd (34 cm) of accent fabric
- ☐ Eight 9/16" (14 mm) dia. buttons

For Pinwheel Tote, you will also need:
- ☐ 45 charm squares for front, back, sides, bottom, and handle*
- ☐ Two 1 1/8" (29 mm) dia. buttons

*A fat quarter can be substituted for 9 charm squares for the sides and bottom of the tote.

Pocket Tote

Charms-On-Point Tote

CUTTING THE PIECES

*Follow **Rotary Cutting**, page 40, **Cutting Charts**, and **Cutting Diagram**, to cut fabric. All measurements include ¼" seam allowances.*

Cutting Chart (for all totes)

PIECE(S)	FABRIC	SIZE	CUT
cuff	#1	18½" x 7"	2
lining	#2	18½" x 16¼"	2
inside pocket	#2	18½" x 12"	2
lining	fusible interfacing	18½" x 16¼"	2
front/back	fusible fleece	14" x 14"	2
side/bottom	fusible fleece	14" x 5"	3
cuff	fusible fleece	18½" x 3"	2
handle	fusible fleece*	23" x 5"	2
drawstring closure (optional)	#3	18½" x 9"	2

*The handles are quite thick. You may choose to use interfacing or a lighter weight fleece for the handles.

Cutting Chart (for Charms-On-Point Tote)

PIECE(S)	FABRIC	SIZE	CUT
short sashing	accent fabric	1" x 5"	12
long sashing	accent fabric	1" x 15"	4
corners	accent fabric	7" x 7"	2

Fusible Fleece Cutting Diagram

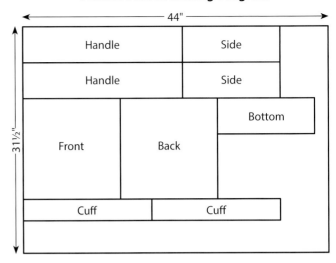

MAKING THE FRONT AND BACK

*Follow the instructions for your desired tote front and back. Follow **Sewing**, page 41, and **Pressing**, page 42, to make tote. Match right sides and use ¼" seam allowances unless otherwise indicated.*

Pocket Tote

1. For pocket, sew 2 assorted **charm squares** together along 1 edge. Turn right side out; press.
2. Press sewn edge down 1".
3. Place pocket on 1 square and baste in place ⅛" from sides and bottom to make **Unit 1**. Make 2 Unit 1's.

Unit 1 (make 2)

4. Sew 3 assorted charm squares together to make **Unit 2**. Make 4 Unit 2's.

Unit 2 (make 4)

5. Sew 1 assorted charm square on each side of Unit 1 to make **Unit 3**. Make 2 Unit 3's.

Unit 3 (make 2)

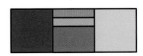

6. Sew 2 Unit 2's and 1 Unit 3 together to make **front**. Repeat to make **back**.

Front/Back

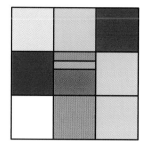

Charms-On-Point Tote

1. Sew 2 **short sashings** and 3 assorted charm squares together to make **Unit 4**. Make 6 Unit 4's.

Unit 4 (make 6)

2. Sew 2 **long sashings** and 3 Unit 4's together to make **Unit 5**. Make 2 Unit 5's.

Unit 5 (make 2)

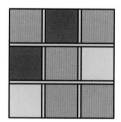

3. Cut each **corner** *twice* diagonally *(Fig. 1)* to make 8 **corner triangles**.

Fig. 1

4. Center and sew long edges of corner triangles to sides of Unit 5 *(Fig. 2)*. Press triangles outward *(Fig. 3)*. The triangles are oversized and will be trimmed later.

Fig. 2   Fig. 3

5. Rotate piece 45°. Trimming an even amount from all sides, trim piece to a square 14" x 14" *(Fig. 4)* to make **front**.

Fig. 4   Front

6. Repeat Steps 4-5 to make **back**.

Pinwheel Tote

1. Fold 1 charm square to make a **Prairie Point**. Make 8 Prairie Points.

Prairie Point (make 8)

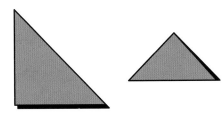

2. Sew 1 Prairie Point to 1 charm square to make a **Prairie Point Square**. Make 8 Prairie Point Squares. Trim triangle points even with sides of charm square to eliminate bulk.

Prairie Point Square (make 8)

3. Sew 2 Prairie Point Squares together to make **Unit 6**. Make 4 Unit 6's. Press seam allowances open.

Unit 6 (make 4)

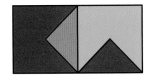

4. Sew 2 Unit 6's together to make a **Prairie Point Block**. Stitch across intersection again to reinforce the center seam. Pick out a couple of stitches in the seam allowances to allow the seam allowances to lie in opposite directions. Make 2 Prairie Point Blocks.

Prairie Point Block (make 2)

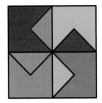

5. Sew 2 charm squares together to make **Unit 7**. Make 2 Unit 7's.

Unit 7 (make 2)

6. Sew 1 Unit 7 to left side of Prairie Point Block to make **Unit 8**. Make 2 Unit 8's.

Unit 8 (make 2)

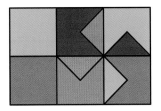

7. Sew 3 charm squares together to make **Unit 9**. Make 2 Unit 9's.

Unit 9 (make 2)

8. Sew 1 Unit 9 to 1 Unit 8 to make **front**. Repeat to make **back**.

Front/Back

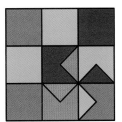

MAKING THE SIDES AND BOTTOM

1. Sew 3 charm squares together to make 1 **side**. Repeat to make another side and 1 **bottom**. You may substitute 3 rectangles 5" x 14", cut from fat quarters.

MAKING THE HANDLES

1. Sew 5 charm squares together side by side to make 1 **handle**.
2. Follow manufacturer's instructions to fuse the wrong side of 1 handle on the fusible side of 1 **fusible fleece handle**. Repeat for remaining handle.
3. Matching *wrong* sides and long edges, press handle in half; unfold.
4. Press long raw edges of handle to meet the center crease.
5. Matching folded edges, fold handle in half; press.
6. Pin edges together. Sewing through all layers, sew handle close to each edge. Sew additional stitching lines if desired for a decorative effect.
7. Repeat Steps 1-6 for remaining handle.

MAKING THE CUFF

1. Matching *wrong* sides, fold **cuff** in half lengthwise; press.
2. Unfold the cuff and place the fusible side of the **cuff fleece** on the wrong side of the fabric, aligning 1 long edge of the fleece with the fold of the fabric. Refold the cuff and fuse fleece in place.
3. Repeat Steps 1-2 to make a second cuff.
4. Unfold the cuff pieces again. Matching fleece-covered areas, sew short edges together. Press seam allowances open. Refold the cuff.

Optional Drawstring Closure

MAKING THE DRAWSTRING CLOSURE (OPTIONAL FOR ALL TOTES)

1. Beginning 2" from edge (top) on one end only, sew **drawstring closure** pieces together along short sides *(Fig. 5)*.

Fig. 5

2. Press the seam allowances open, pressing the unsewn area ¼" to wrong side.
3. To form casing, fold top edge ¼" to inside; press 1" to inside again. Sew close to each folded edge.

MAKING THE LINING AND INSIDE POCKETS

1. Matching *wrong* sides, fold 1 **inside pocket** in half lengthwise so that pocket is 6" x 18½". Repeat with remaining inside pocket.
2. Place the fusible side of 1 **fusible interfacing lining** on the wrong side of 1 **lining**. Follow manufacturer's instructions to fuse.

3. Draw a horizontal line across lining 3" from 1 long edge of tote (bottom).

4. With folded edge of inside pocket pointing downward, match raw edges of pocket to drawn line *(Fig. 6)*; pin. Sew pocket in place ¼" from edge.

Fig. 6

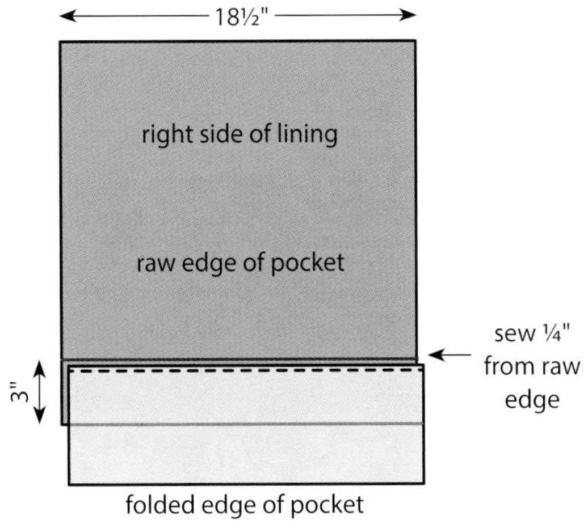

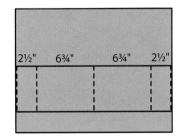

18½"

right side of lining

raw edge of pocket

sew ¼" from raw edge

3"

folded edge of pocket

5. Press pocket up and baste at each side. Sew vertical lines to create pocket dividers *(Fig. 7)*.

Fig. 7

2½" 6¾" 6¾" 2½"

6. Refer to **Fig. 8** to cut a 2¼" notch from each bottom corner.

Fig. 8

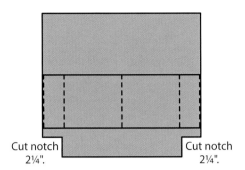

Cut notch 2¼".   Cut notch 2¼".

7. Repeat Steps 2-6 to make remaining lining piece.

8. Matching pockets and leaving a 6" opening for turning, sew lining pieces together along each side and the bottom (**Fig. 9**).

Fig. 9

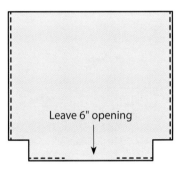

Leave 6" opening

9. To box the bottom, match right sides and align side seam with bottom seam; sew across ends (**Fig. 10**).

Fig. 10

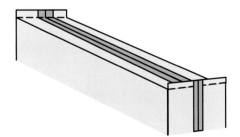

ASSEMBLING THE TOTE

1. Place wrong side of tote front on fusible side of **fusible fleece front**; fuse. Topstitch around each square, if desired. Repeat with tote back.
2. Sew buttons to tote front and back.
3. Place wrong side of **bottom** on fusible side of **fusible fleece bottom**; fuse. Topstitch around each square, if desired. If using a rectangle instead of charm squares, quilt as desired. Repeat with each side.
4. Stopping and backstitching ¼" from bottom edge, sew sides to front of tote.
5. Stopping and backstitching ¼" from bottom edge, sew sides to back of tote.
6. Stopping and backstitching ¼" from each corner, sew bottom to front, back, and sides of tote.
7. Trim corners and turn tote right side out.
8. Matching raw edges and side seams, sew cuff to right side of tote body.
9. Pin raw edges of 1 handle even with top edge and 6" from side seams over cuff *(Fig. 11)*; baste in place. Sew again to reinforce seam. Repeat for remaining handle on tote back.

Fig. 11

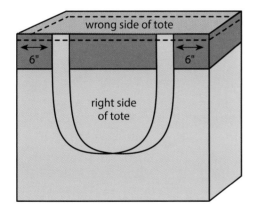

10. If adding drawstring closure, match raw edges and sew right side of **drawstring closure** to right side of tote body with cuff and handles sandwiched in between.
11. Matching right sides, place tote body into lining with cuff, handle, and optional drawstring closure sandwiched in between. Aligning top raw edges and side seams, stitch around top *(Fig. 12)*.

Fig. 12

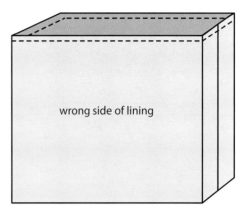

12. Turn tote right side out through the opening in the lining. Hand stitch opening closed. Tuck lining and optional drawstring closure into tote. Turn cuff up out of the way. Topstitch around top of tote. The handles are thick; sew slowly to avoid breaking the needle.
13. Thread drawstring through casing.

OPTIONAL STURDY BOTTOM

Cut 2 pieces of mat board 4½" x 13½"; glue together. Cut two 5¼" x 14¼" fabric pieces. Matching right sides, place fabric pieces together. Sew along 2 long edges and 1 short edge; turn right side out. Press raw edges ¼" to wrong side; press ¼" to wrong side again. Insert mat board into case. To close, stitch along folded edges.

Instructions are given for 3 larger bags and 3 smaller bags. You can choose from a variety of widths, heights, and depths. The pattern also gives you 3 options for the front and back of the bag. Strips or charm squares can be substituted for the color-block front and back.

The Big Shopper

Designs by Sue Marsh

FINISHED SIZES

	LARGER BAGS		SMALLER BAGS
A	18½"w x 15"h x 4½"d (47 cm x 38 cm x 11 cm)	**D**	16½"w x 15"h x 4½"d (42 cm x 38 cm x 11 cm)
B	17"w x 16"h x 6"d (43 cm x 41 cm x 15 cm)	**E**	15"w x 16"h x 6"d (38 cm x 41 cm x 15 cm)
C	14"w x 14½"h x 9"d (36 cm x 37 cm x 23 cm)	**F**	12"w x 14½"h x 9"d (30 cm x 37 cm x 23 cm)

....

SHOPPING LIST

Yardage is based on 43"/44" (109 cm/112 cm) wide fabric with a usable width of 40" (102 cm).

- ☐ ⅜ yd (34 cm) of fabric #1 for top band
- ☐ ⅛ yd (11 cm) of fabric #2 for accent strip
- ☐ 12" x 12" (30 cm x 30 cm) square of fabric #3 for circle
- ☐ ⅞ yd (80 cm) of fabric #4 for bag body*
- ☐ 5" x 10" (13 cm x 25 cm) piece of fabric #5 for letter appliqués
- ☐ 1½ yds (1.4 m) of fabric #6 for lining and inside pockets (If using directional fabric, you will need 2 yds [1.8 m].)
- ☐ ¼ yd (23 cm) of fabric #7 for handle**
- ☐ 2 yds (1.8 m) of 44"/45" (112 cm/114 cm) wide single-sided fusible fleece (such as The Warm Company® Warm Fleece™ or Pellon® #987F)
- ☐ Sixteen ⅝" (16 mm) buttons (optional, if using charm squares)
- ☐ Paper-backed fusible web
- ☐ Stabilizer
- ☐ Water-soluble fabric marking pen

* Twelve assorted 2½" (6.35 cm) wide strips or 30 assorted 5" x 5" (12.7 cm x 12.7 cm) charm squares can be substituted for the bag body fabric.

**22 assorted rectangles 2½" x 5" (6.35 cm x 12.7 cm) can be substituted for the handle fabric.

CUTTING THE PIECES

Follow Rotary Cutting, page 40, and Cutting Charts, to cut fabric. Wof refers to width of fabric.
All measurements include ¼" seam allowances.

Cutting Chart (Larger Bags)

PIECE(S)	FABRIC	SIZE	CUT
top band	#1	23" x 5"	2
accent strip	#2	23" x 1½"	2
circle	#3	use circle pattern, page 39	4
bag body	#4	23" x 14"	2
		or	
		5" x 5" charm squares	30
		or	
		strips 2½"w x wof	12
lining	#6	23" x 19½"	2
inside pocket	#6	23" x 12"	2
handle	#7	5" x wof	1
		or	
		rectangles 2½" x 5"	22
bag body	fusible fleece	23" x 19½"	4
handle	fusible fleece	5" x wof	1
inside pocket	fusible fleece	23" x 5½"	2
circle	fusible fleece	use circle pattern, page 39	2

Cutting Chart (Smaller Bags)

PIECE(S)	FABRIC	SIZE	CUT
top band	#1	21" x 5"	2
accent strip	#2	21" x 1½"	2
circle	#3	use circle pattern, page 39	4
bag body	#4	21" x 14" **or**	2
		5" x 5" charm squares **or**	30
		strips 2½"w x wof	12
lining	#6	21" x 19½"	2
inside pocket	#6	21" x 12"	2
handle	#7	5" x wof **or**	1
		rectangles 2½" x 5"	22
bag body	fusible fleece	21" x 19½"	4
handle	fusible fleece	5" x wof	1
inside pocket	fusible fleece	21" x 5½"	2
circle	fusible fleece	use circle pattern, page 39	2

CUTTING THE APPLIQUÉS

From fabric #5 for letter appliqué:

• Find a font you like on the computer. Size desired letter to approximately 3½" tall; print. Using printed letter for pattern, refer to **Preparing Fusible Appliqués**, page 45, to cut desired letter.

HELPFUL MEASUREMENTS

Use the following measurements to determine the size to cut the corner notch for boxing the bag bottom, the placement of the inside pockets, and what size to make the optional sturdy bottom for the various size bags.

FINISHED BAG SIZE	NOTCH SIZE	POCKET ALIGNMENT LINE	BAG BOTTOM SIZE
Larger Bags			
18½"w x 15"h x 4½"d	2¼" x 2¼"	16¼" from top	18½" x 4½"
17"w x 16"h x 6"d	3" x 3"	15½" from top	17" x 6"
14"w x 14½"h x 9"d	4½" x 4½"	14" from top	14" x 9"
Smaller Bags			
16½"w x 15"h x 4½"d	2¼" x 2¼"	16¼" from top	16½" x 4½"
15"w x 16"h x 6"d	3" x 3"	15½" from top	15" x 6"
12"w x 14½"h x 9"d	4½" x 4½"	14" from top	12" x 9"

MAKING THE BAG BODY

*Follow **Sewing**, page 41, and **Pressing**, page 42, using the pieces cut for your desired size bag. Dimensions for smaller sizes are shown in parentheses. Match right sides and use ¼" seam allowances unless otherwise indicated.*

1. There are 3 options for the bag body. The **bag body** given in the cutting list can be used or the bag body can be pieced from charm squares or strips.

   If using charm squares for bag body, sew 5 **charm squares** together to make a row. Make 3 Rows. Sew the rows together to make a 23" x 14" bag body front for larger bags. For smaller bags, trim the rectangle to 21" x 14". Repeat for bag body back of corresponding size.

   If using strips for bag body, sew 12 **strips** together along long edges. From this piece, cut 2 rectangles 23" x 14" (21" x 14") for bag body front and back.

2. Refer to **Fig. 1** to sew 1 top band, 1 accent strip, and 1 bag body front together to make bag front.

Fig. 1

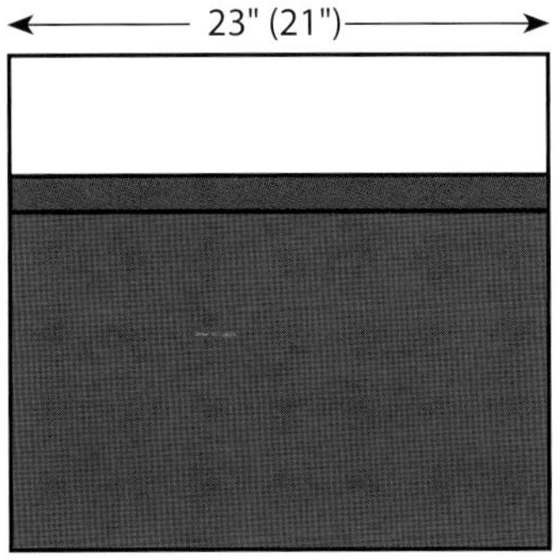

23" (21")

3. Place wrong side of bag front on fusible side of **fusible fleece bag body**. Follow manufacturer's instructions to fuse. If desired, topstitch along each seamline or around each square through all layers. For charm square bag, sew 1 button at the intersection of each group of 4 squares.

4. Repeat Steps 2-3 to make bag back.

5. Center and fuse 1 letter on 1 **fabric circle**. Refer to **Machine Applique**, page 45, to stitch letter in place using a narrow satin stitch or a blanket stitch.

6. Place wrong side of letter circle on fusible side of **fusible fleece circle**; fuse.

7. Cut a 2" slit in the center of another fabric circle.

8. Matching right sides, layer letter circle and slit circle together. Sew around outer edge of circles. Turn circle right side out through slit; press.

9. Refer to **Fig. 2** to position circle on bag front; pin. Sew circle in place using a narrow satin stitch or a blanket stitch.

Fig. 2

10. Repeat Steps 5-9 to sew circle to bag back.

11. Referring to **Helpful Measurements** to determine notch size, cut a notch *(Fig. 3)* from each bottom corner of front and back.

Fig. 3

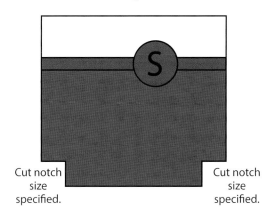

Cut notch size specified.　　　Cut notch size specified.

12. Sew front and back together along each side and the bottom.

13. To box the bottom, match right sides and align side seams with bottom seam; sew across ends *(Fig. 4)*.

Fig. 4

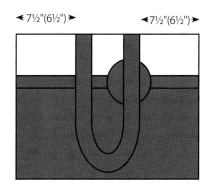

MAKING AND ATTACHING THE HANDLES

1. There are 2 options for the handles. The handles can be made from a single strip or from assorted small fabric pieces.
   If using assorted small fabric pieces, match long edges and sew 22 **rectangles** together to make a handle.

2. Place the wrong side of handle on the fusible side of **fusible fleece handle**; fuse.

3. Matching *wrong* sides, press handle in half; unfold. Press long raw edges of handle to meet center crease.

4. Matching folded edges, fold handle in half; press.

5. Pin edges together. Sewing through all layers, sew handle close to each edge. Sew additional stitching lines if desired for a decorative effect.

6. Cut handle in half to make 2 handles.

7. Pin raw edges of 1 handle even with top edge and 7½" (6½") from side seams on right side of bag back *(Fig. 5)*; baste in place. Repeat for remaining handle on bag front.

Fig. 5

◄7½"(6½")►　　　◄7½"(6½")►

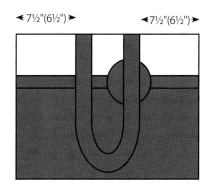

MAKING THE INSIDE POCKETS

1. Matching wrong sides, fold **inside pocket** in half lengthwise so that pocket is 23" (21") x 6".
2. Unfold the pocket and place the fusible side of the corresponding **fusible fleece inside pocket** on the wrong side of the fabric, aligning 1 long edge of the fleece with the fold of the fabric. Refold the pocket and fuse fleece in place.
3. Repeat Steps 1-2 to make another inside pocket.

MAKING THE LINING

1. Place the wrong side of 1 **lining** on the fusible side of 1 **fusible fleece bag body** and fuse.
2. Refer to **Helpful Measurements** to draw pocket alignment line across lining parallel with top edge of bag. With folded edge of inside pocket pointing downward, match raw edges of pocket to drawn line *(Fig. 6)*; pin. Sew pocket in place ¼" from edge.

Fig. 6

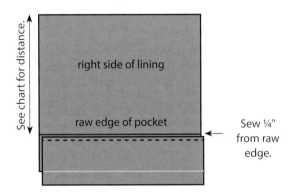

3. Press pocket up and baste at each side. Sew vertical lines to create pocket dividers *(Fig. 7)*. Referring to **Helpful Measurements** to determine notch size, cut a notch from each bottom corner of front and back lining.

Fig. 7

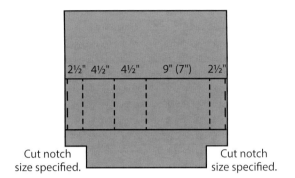

4. Repeat Steps 1-3 to make remaining lining piece.
5. Matching pockets and leaving a 6" opening for turning, sew lining pieces together along each side and the bottom *(Fig. 8)*.

Fig. 8

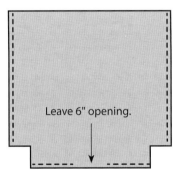

6. To box the bottom, match right sides and align side seam with bottom seam; sew across ends *(see Fig. 4)*.

ASSEMBLING THE BAG

1. Matching right sides, place the bag inside the lining with the handle sandwiched in between. Aligning top raw edges and matching side seams, sew raw edges together around top *(Fig. 9)*.

Fig. 9

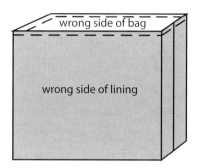

2. Turn bag right side out through opening. Hand stitch opening closed. Push lining into bag. Topstitch around top of bag if desired.

OPTIONAL STURDY BOTTOM

Refer to **Helpful Measurements** to cut 2 pieces of mat board the size of the bag bottom - ½"; glue together. Cut two pieces of scrap fabric the size of the bag bottom + ½". Matching right sides, place fabric pieces together. Sew along 2 long edges and 1 short edge; turn right side out. Press raw edges ¼" to wrong side; press ¼" to wrong side again. Insert mat board into case. To close, stitch along fold.

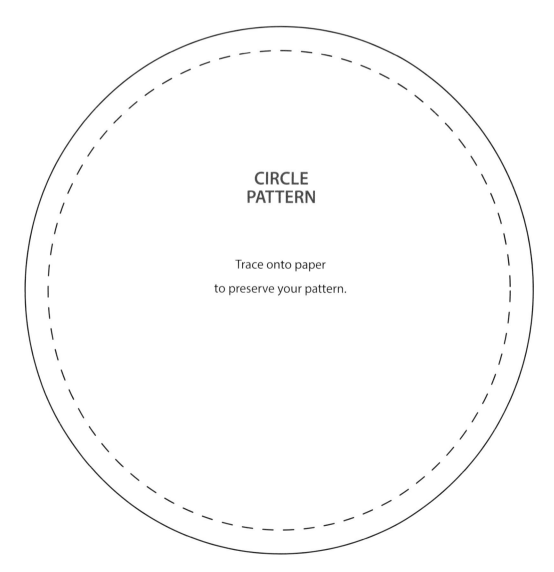

CIRCLE
PATTERN

Trace onto paper

to preserve your pattern.

General Instructions

To make your sewing and quilting easier and more enjoyable, we encourage you to carefully read all of the general instructions, study the color photographs, and familiarize yourself with the individual project instructions before beginning a project.

FABRICS

SELECTING FABRICS
Choose high-quality, medium-weight 100% cotton fabrics. All-cotton fabrics hold a crease better, fray less, and are easier to quilt than cotton/polyester blends. Yardage requirements listed for each project are based on 43"/44" wide fabric with a "usable" width of 40" after shrinkage and trimming selvages. Actual usable width will probably vary slightly from fabric to fabric. Our recommended yardage lengths should be adequate for occasional re-squaring of fabric when many cuts are required.

PREPARING FABRICS
We recommend that all fabrics be washed, dried, and pressed before cutting. If fabrics are not pre-washed, washing the finished project will cause shrinkage and give it a more "antiqued" look and feel. Bright and dark colors, which may run, should always be washed before cutting. After washing and drying fabric, fold lengthwise with wrong sides together and matching selvages.

ROTARY CUTTING
Most of the pieces for the projects are rotary cut. In many cases you will make a first cut across the width of the fabric, then cut that strip into the final size(s).

- Make all cuts from the selvage-to-selvage width of the fabric unless otherwise indicated in project instructions.

- Place fabric on work surface with fold closest to you.

- Square left edge of fabric using rotary cutter and rulers (**Figs. 1 - 2**).

Fig. 1

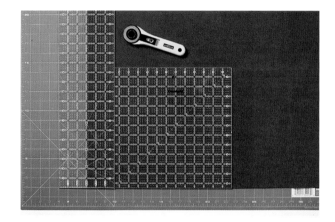

Fig. 2

- To cut each strip required for a project, place ruler over cut edge of fabric, aligning desired marking on ruler with cut edge; make cut (**Fig. 3**).

Fig. 3

- When cutting several strips from a single piece of fabric, it is important to make sure that cuts remain at a perfect right angle to the fold; square fabric as needed.
- Remove selvage edges before sub-cutting strips to final sizes.

SEWING

Precise cutting, followed by accurate sewing, will ensure that all pieces of your project fit together well.

- Set sewing machine stitch length for approximately 11 stitches per inch.

- Use a matching or neutral-colored 100% cotton sewing thread (not quilting thread) in needle and in bobbin.

- An accurate seam allowance is essential.

- When sewing, always place pieces right sides together and match raw edges, unless otherwise indicated; pin if necessary.

PIECING

Sewing small fabric shapes, such as squares, triangles, or rectangles, together to form larger shapes is called Piecing. For example, the pockets of the **Shoulder Bag**, page 7, are pieced. Piecing requires the use of some specific techniques not usually found in basic sewing.

Trimming Points

Trim away points of any seam allowances that extend beyond edges of sewn pieces (**Fig. 4**).

Fig. 4

Sewing Across Seam Intersections

When sewing across intersection of two seams, place pieces right sides together and match seams exactly, making sure seam allowances are pressed in opposite directions (**Fig. 5**).

Fig. 5

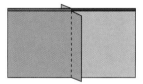

Sewing Sharp Points

To ensure sharp points when joining triangular or diagonal pieces, stitch across the center of the "X" (shown in pink) formed on wrong side by previous seams (**Fig. 6**).

Fig. 6

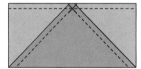

Making Triangle-Squares

This method reduces handling of the bias edges that is normally required when triangles are cut then sewn.

1. Matching right sides and raw edges, place two squares together. On the wrong side of the lighter colored square, draw a diagonal line across the square (**Fig. 7**).

Fig. 7

2.   Sew ¼" from each side of drawn line (**Fig. 8**).

Fig. 8

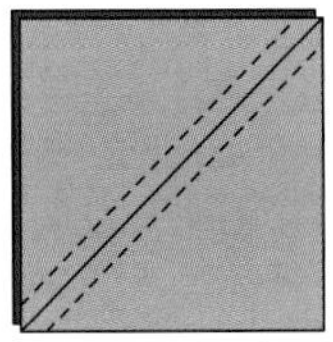

3.   Cut on drawn line to make 2 **Triangle-Squares** (**Fig. 9**).

Fig. 9

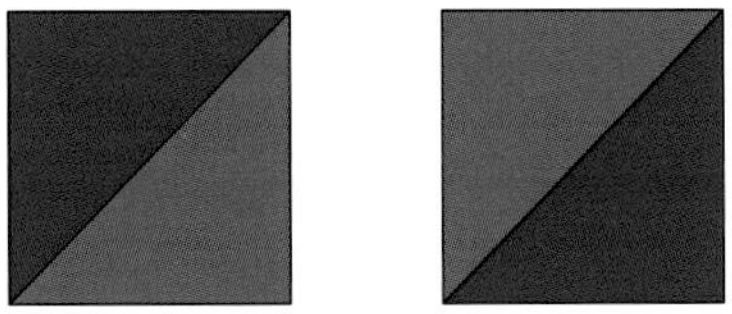

4.   Press seam allowances toward darker fabric and trim, if needed, to the size given in project instructions (**Fig. 10**).

Fig. 10

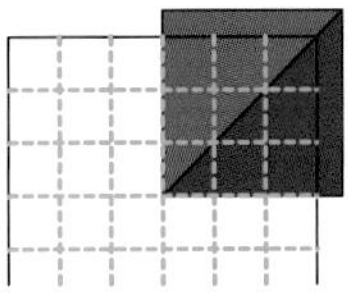

PRESSING

•   Use steam iron set on "Cotton" for all pressing.

•   Press after sewing each seam.

PRESSING WHEN PIECING

•   Seam allowances are almost always pressed to one side, usually toward darker fabric. However, to reduce bulk it may occasionally be necessary to press seam allowances toward the lighter fabric or even to press them open.

•   To prevent dark fabric seam allowances from showing through light fabric, it may occasionally be necessary to trim darker seam allowance slightly narrower than lighter seam allowance.

MAKING QUILTED FABRIC

Quilting holds the three layers (outer fabric, batting, and lining) of a quilt "sandwich" together. Our projects are machine quilted. Please read entire **Making Quilted Fabric** section, pages 42 – 43, before beginning project.

MARKING QUILTING LINES

Quilting lines may be marked using fabric marking pencils, chalk markers, water- or air-soluble pens, or lead pencils.

Simple quilting designs may be marked with chalk or chalk pencil after making the quilt sandwich. A small area may be marked, then quilted, before moving to next area to be marked. Intricate designs should be marked before making the quilt sandwich using a more durable marker.

Caution: Pressing may permanently set some marks. **Test** different markers **on scrap fabric** to find one that marks clearly and can be thoroughly removed.

MAKING THE QUILT SANDWICH

1.   Cover work area with paper or plastic to prevent damage from overspray.

2.   Position **lining** wrong side up on a flat work surface. Following manufacturer's instructions, spray lining lightly with quilt basting spray. Place **batting** over lining and smooth pieces together.

3.   Lightly spray wrong side of **outer fabric** with quilt basting spray. Position outer fabric, right side up, over batting and smooth pieces together. Press layers together firmly with your hands.

MACHINE QUILTING METHODS

Thread the needle with general-purpose thread that matches the outer fabric to make quilting lines blend with the outer fabric or use a decorative thread, such as a variegated, a metallic, or a contrasting-color general-purpose thread, to make quilting lines stand out more. Use general-purpose thread in bobbin. **Do not** use quilting thread.

Tip: When quilting, start in the middle of the quilt sandwich and work your way to the outer edges.

Straight-Line Quilting

The term "straight-line" is somewhat deceptive, since curves (especially gentle ones) as well as straight lines can be stitched with this technique.

1. Set stitch length for six to ten stitches per inch and attach walking foot to sewing machine.
2. Determine which section of the quilt sandwich will have longest continuous quilting line, oftentimes this will be from corner to corner when crosshatching. Roll up and secure each edge of a large quilt sandwich to help reduce the bulk. Smaller quilt sandwiches may not need to be rolled.
3. Begin stitching on longest quilting line, using very short stitches for the first ¼" to "lock" quilting. Stitch across quilt sandwich, using one hand on each side of walking foot to slightly spread fabric and to guide fabric through machine. Lock stitches at end of quilting line.
4. Continue machine quilting, stitching longer quilting lines first to stabilize the quilt sandwich before moving on to other areas.

Free-Motion Quilting

Free-motion quilting may be free form or may follow a marked pattern. Meandering is a type of free-motion quilting.

1. Attach darning foot to sewing machine and lower or cover feed dogs.
2. Position quilt sandwich under the darning foot; lower foot. Holding top thread, take a stitch and pull bobbin thread to top of quilt sandwich. To "lock" beginning of quilting line, hold top and bobbin threads while making three to five stitches in place.
3. Use one hand on each side of darning foot to slightly spread fabric and to move quilt sandwich through the machine. Even stitch length is achieved by using smooth, flowing hand motion and steady machine speed. Slow machine speed and fast hand movement will create long stitches. Fast machine speed and slow hand movement will create short stitches. Move quilt sandwich sideways, back and forth, in a circular motion, or in a random motion to create desired designs; do not rotate quilt sandwich. Lock stitches at end of each quilting line.

BINDING

Binding is used to cover raw edges to give a finished look to your project.

MAKING BINDING

1. Use the diagonal seams method (**Fig. 11**), to sew binding strips together end to end to make 1 continuous binding strip.

Fig. 11

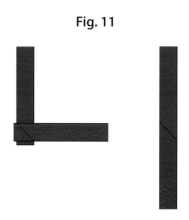

2. Matching wrong sides and raw edges, press strips in half lengthwise to complete binding.

ATTACHING BINDING

For any of the following methods of attaching binding, you will first sew the raw edges of the binding to the "wrong" or lining side of the project and bring the folded edge to the "right" or outer fabric side and topstitch in place (**Fig. 12**).

Fig. 12

Sometimes this is obvious like the binding along the top edge of the pocket on the **Shoulder Bag**, page 7. The lining is the wrong side and the outer fabric is the right side. Other times the right and wrong sides are not quite as apparent such as around the flap and outer edges of the **Mini Bag**, page 3. In this case, the outer fabric of the side and the lining of the flap would be the wrong side and the outer fabric of the project body is the right side. When binding seams on the inside of a project, it doesn't matter which side of the seam allowance you use as the right side.

ATTACHING CONTINUOUS BINDING

Continuous Binding has no easily visible beginning or end and is used around the edges of a bag, backpack, or tote.

1. Press 1 end of binding diagonally (**Fig. 13**).

Fig. 13

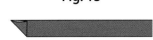

2. Beginning on wrong/lining side of project with the pressed end of binding, match raw edges of project and binding and pin binding around raw edge of project.
3. Using a ¼" seam allowance, sew binding to project, until binding overlaps beginning end by about 2". Trim excess binding.
4. Fold binding to right side, covering stitching line and pin in place.
5. Topstitch binding in place close to folded edge.

ATTACHING OPEN END BINDING

Open End Binding is used when the raw ends of a bound edge will be caught in a seam or covered by another strip of binding.

1. Matching raw edges of binding to raw edge of project, pin a length of binding along one edge. Using a ¼" seam allowance, sew binding to project (**Fig. 14**).

Fig. 14

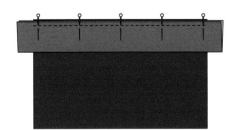

2. Fold binding over seam allowance, covering stitching line, and pin pressed edge in place (**Fig. 15**).

Fig. 15

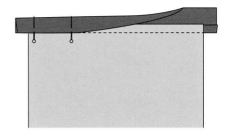

3. Topstitch binding in place close to pressed edge.
4. Trim raw ends of binding even with edges.

ATTACHING CLOSED END BINDING

Closed End Binding is used when the seam to be bound will not be caught or covered by another seam.

1. Matching raw edges and leaving approximately ½" of binding extending at end(s), pin a length of binding along one edge (**Fig. 16**).

Fig. 16

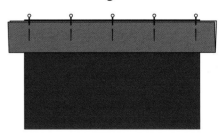

2. Using a ¼" seam allowance, sew binding to project (**Fig. 17**).

Fig. 17

3. Fold under raw end(s) of binding (**Fig. 18**); pin in place. Fold binding over seam allowance, covering stitching line, and pin pressed edge in place (**Fig. 19**).

Fig. 18

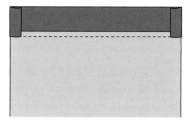

Fig. 19

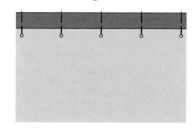

4. Topstitch binding in place close to pressed edge.

MACHINE APPLIQUÉ
PREPARING FUSIBLE APPLIQUÉS

White or light-colored fabrics may need to be lined with fusible interfacing before applying fusible web to prevent darker fabrics from showing through.

1. Place paper-backed fusible web, paper side up, over appliqué pattern. Trace pattern onto paper side of web with pencil as many times as indicated in project instructions for a single fabric.
2. Follow manufacturer's instructions to fuse traced patterns to wrong side of fabrics. Do not remove paper backing.
3. Use scissors to cut out appliqué pieces along traced lines. Remove paper backing from all pieces.

SATIN STITCH APPLIQUÉ

A good satin stitch is a thick, smooth, almost solid line of zigzag stitching that covers the exposed raw edges of appliqué pieces.

1. Pin stabilizer, such as paper or any of the commercially available products, on wrong side of background fabric before stitching appliqués in place.
2. Thread sewing machine with general-purpose thread; use general-purpose thread that matches background fabric in bobbin.
3. Set sewing machine for a medium (approximately ⅛") zigzag stitch and a short stitch length. Slightly loosening the top tension may yield a smoother stitch.
4. Begin by stitching two or three stitches in place (drop feed dogs or set stitch length at 0) to anchor thread. Most of the Satin Stitch should be on the appliqué with the right edge of the stitch falling at the outside edge of the appliqué. Stitch over all exposed raw edges of appliqué pieces.
5. (**Note:** Dots on **Figs. 20-25** indicate where to leave needle in fabric when pivoting.) For outside corners, stitch just past corner, stopping with needle in background fabric (**Fig. 20**). Raise presser foot. Pivot project, lower presser foot, and stitch adjacent side (**Fig. 21**).

Fig. 20	**Fig. 21**

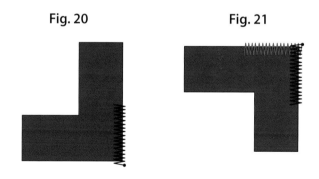

6. For inside corners, stitch just past corner, stopping with needle in appliqué fabric (**Fig. 22**). Raise presser foot. Pivot project, lower presser foot, and stitch adjacent side (**Fig. 23**).

Fig. 22   **Fig. 23**

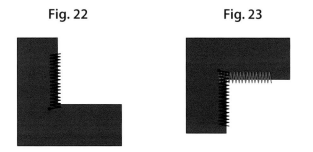

7. When stitching outside curves, stop with needle in background fabric. Raise presser foot and pivot project as needed. Lower presser foot and continue stitching, pivoting as often as necessary to follow curve (**Fig. 24**).

Fig. 24

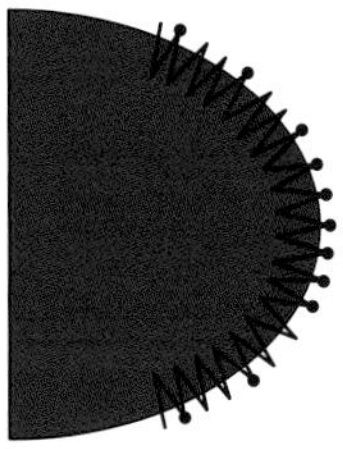

8. When stitching inside curves, stop with needle in appliqué fabric. Raise presser foot and pivot project as needed. Lower presser foot and continue stitching, pivoting as often as necessary to follow curve (**Fig. 25**).

Fig. 25

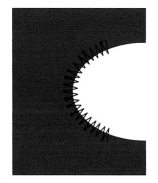

9. Do not backstitch at end of stitching. Pull threads to wrong side of background fabric; knot thread and trim ends.
10. Carefully tear away stabilizer.

BLANKET STITCH APPLIQUÉ

Some sewing machines are capable of a Blanket Stitch. Refer to your owner's manual for machine set-up. If your machine does not have this stitch, try any of the decorative stitches your machine has until you are satisfied with the look.

1. Thread sewing machine and bobbin with 100% cotton thread in desired weight.
2. Attach an open-toe presser foot. Select far right needle position and needle down (if your machine has these features).
3. If desired, pin a stabilizer, such as paper or any of the commercially available products on wrong side of background fabric before stitching appliqués in place.
4. Bring bobbin thread to the top of the fabric by lowering then raising the needle, bringing up the bobbin thread loop. Pull the loop all the way to the surface.
5. Begin by stitching two or three stitches in place (drop feed dogs or set stitch length at 0), or use your machine's lock stitch feature, if equipped, to anchor thread. Return setting to selected Blanket Stitch.
6. Most of the Blanket Stitch should be on the appliqué with the right edges of the stitch falling at the very outside edge of the appliqué. Stitch over all exposed raw edges of appliqué pieces.

7. (*Note:* Dots on **Figs. 26-30** indicate where to leave needle in fabric when pivoting.) Always stopping with needle down in background fabric, refer to **Fig. 26** to stitch outside points like tips of leaves. Stop one stitch short of point. Raise presser foot. Pivot project slightly, lower presser foot, and make an angled Stitch 1. Take next stitch, stop at point, and pivot so Stitch 2 will be perpendicular to point. Pivot slightly to make Stitch 3. Continue stitching.

Fig. 26

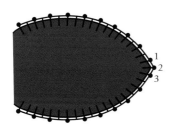

8. For outside corners (**Fig. 27**), stitch to corner, stopping with needle in background fabric. Raise presser foot. Pivot project, lower presser foot, and take an angled stitch. Raise presser foot. Pivot project, lower presser foot and stitch adjacent side.

Fig. 27

9. For inside corners (**Fig. 28**), stitch to the corner, taking the last bite at corner and stopping with the needle down in background fabric. Raise presser foot. Pivot project, lower presser foot, and take an angled stitch. Raise presser foot. Pivot project, lower presser foot and stitch adjacent side.

Fig. 28

10. When stitching outside curves (**Fig. 29**), stop with needle down in background fabric. Raise presser foot and pivot project as needed. Lower presser foot and continue stitching, pivoting as often as necessary to follow curve. Small circles may require pivoting between each stitch.

Fig. 29

11. When stitching inside curves (**Fig. 30**), stop with needle down in background fabric. Raise presser foot and pivot project as needed. Lower presser foot and continue stitching, pivoting as often as necessary to follow curve.

Fig. 30

12. When stopping stitching, use a lock stitch to sew 5 or 6 stitches in place or use a needle to pull threads to wrong side of background fabric (**Fig. 31**); knot, then trim ends.

Fig. 31

13. Carefully tear away stabilizer, if used.

Metric Conversion Chart

Inches x 2.54 = centimeters (cm)
Inches x 25.4 = millimeters (mm)
Inches x .0254 = meters (m)

Yards x .9144 = meters (m)
Yards x 91.44 = centimeters (cm)
Centimeters x .3937 = inches (")
Meters x 1.0936 − yards (yd)

Standard Equivalents

1/8"	3.2 mm	0.32 cm	1/8 yard	11.43 cm	0.11 m
1/4"	6.35 mm	0.635 cm	1/4 yard	22.86 cm	0.23 m
3/8"	9.5 mm	0.95 cm	3/8 yard	34.29 cm	0.34 m
1/2"	12.7 mm	1.27 cm	1/2 yard	45.72 cm	0.46 m
5/8"	15.9 mm	1.59 cm	5/8 yard	57.15 cm	0.57 m
3/4"	19.1 mm	1.91 cm	3/4 yard	68.58 cm	0.69 m
7/8"	22.2 mm	2.22 cm	7/8 yard	80 cm	0.8 m
1"	25.4 mm	2.54 cm	1 yard	91.44 cm	0.91 m

We have made every effort to ensure that these instructions are accurate and complete.
We cannot, however, be responsible for human error, typographical mistakes, or variations in individual work.

Production Team: Technical Editor - Lisa Lancaster; Editorial Writer - Susan Frantz Wiles;
Senior Graphic Artist - Lora Puls; Graphic Artist - Kellie McAnulty; Photo Stylists - Angela Alexander
and Lori Wenger; and Photographer - Jason Masters.